WHAT IS SOUND ENERGY?

LAURA LORIA

Britannica®
Educational Publishing

IN ASSOCIATION WITH

ROSEN
EDUCATIONAL SERVICES

Published in 2018 by Britannica Educational Publishing (a trademark of Encyclopædia Britannica, Inc.) in association with The Rosen Publishing Group, Inc.
29 East 21st Street, New York, NY 10010

Distributed exclusively by Rosen Publishing.
To see additional Britannica Educational Publishing titles, go to rosenpublishing.com.

First Edition

Britannica Educational Publishing
J.E. Luebering: Executive Director, Core Editorial
Mary Rose McCudden: Editor, Britannica Student Encyclopedia

Rosen Publishing
Amelie von Zumbusch: Editor
Nelson Sá: Art Director
Nicole Russo-Duco: Designer
Cindy Reiman: Photography Manager
Karen Huang: Photo Researcher

Library of Congress Cataloging-in-Publication Data

Names: Loria, Laura, author.
Title: What is sound energy? / Laura Loria.
Description: First edition. | New York, NY : Britannica Educational Publishing in Association with Rosen Educational Services, 2018. | Series: Let's find out! Forms of energy | Includes bibliographical references and index. | Audience: 1–4.
Identifiers: LCCN 2016058554 | ISBN 9781680487152 (library bound ; alk. paper) | ISBN 9781680487138 (pbk.; alk. paper) | ISBN 9781680487145 (6-pack ; alk. paper)
Subjects: LCSH: Sound—Juvenile literature.
Classification: LCC QC225.5 .L67 2018 | DDC 534—dc23
LC record available at https://lccn.loc.gov/2016058554

Manufactured in the United States of America

Photo credits: Cover, p. 1 Gandee Vasan/Stone/Getty Images; p. 4 ChristineGonsalves/Shutterstock.com; pp. 5, 7, 10, 13, 18 Encyclopædia Britannica, Inc.; p. 6 Svetlana Valoueva/Shutterstock.com; p. 8 LydiaGoolia/iStock/Thinkstock; p. 9 picstodisc/iStock/Thinkstock; p. 11 (left) rck_953/Shutterstock.com, (right) © iStockphoto.com/spooh; p. 12 AdstockRF; p. 14 wavebreakmedia/Shutterstock.com; p. 15 Highwaystarz-Photography/iStock/Thinkstock; p. 16 Kevin Winter/WireImage/Getty Images; p. 17 © iStockphoto.com/People-Images; p. 19 © iStockphoto.com/mixetto; p. 20 kozorog/iStock/Thinkstock; p. 21 Dorling Kindersley/Thinkstock; p. 22 De Agostini Picture Library/De Agostini/Getty Images; p. 23 Steve Kaufman/Corbis Documentary/Getty Images; p. 24 Chad Ehlers/Photographer's Choice/Getty Images; p. 25 Dario Lo Presti/Shutterstock.com; p. 26 © Photos.com/Jupiterimages; p. 27 harleebob/iStock/Thinkstock; p. 28 Kichigin/iStock/Thinkstock; p. 29 Kzenon/Shutterstock.com; interior pages background MoonRock/Shutterstock.com.

CONTENTS

POWER THROUGH MOVEMENT

Have you ever heard someone describe a person by saying he or she has a lot of energy? Usually, when someone says that, they are talking about a person who moves around a lot. It's a good description because things and people need energy to move.

"Energy" is another word for power. It makes things move or work, and makes living things grow.

The shaking movement of a jackhammer produces sound energy. The sound is very loud.

sound waves

Energy can be divided into two categories: potential energy and kinetic energy. Potential energy is power that is stored, to use later. Kinetic energy is power in action, or moving energy.

There are many different kinds of energy, such as electricity, heat, and light. Sound energy is made when an object, or part of an object, **vibrates**. The vibrations move the air around it to make sound waves. These are what we hear.

Sound waves are invisible as they travel through the air from the source of a sound.

VOCABULARY
Something that **vibrates** has a shaking movement.

Have You Heard?

When a dog barks, the sound travels through the air and is received by a human ear.

All sounds travel in the same way. They start at a source, such as a bell that is rung or an object that is hit. A medium, such as air, carries the sound waves. Finally, a receiver detects the sound.

Your receiver is your ear. The human ear has three parts. Each part has its own job. The outer ear collects sound waves and contains

Sound waves move through each of the three parts of the ear before they can be heard.

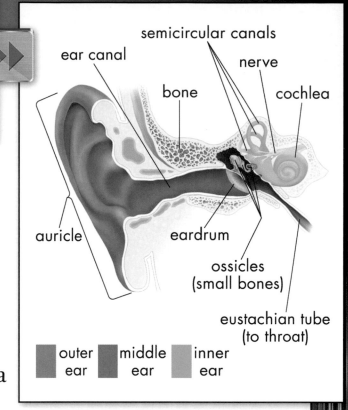

semicircular canals

ear canal

nerve

bone

cochlea

auricle

eardrum

ossicles (small bones)

eustachian tube (to throat)

| outer ear | middle ear | inner ear |

the eardrum. The eardrum vibrates when the waves hit it. The middle ear sends the vibrations to the inner ear over three small bones. Finally, the vibrations go through a fluid in the inner ear, making waves that send a sound signal to your brain.

Sound waves aren't like waves in the ocean, though. They bend in and out quickly, to push and pull the air around them. This movement makes the sounds we hear.

COMPARE AND CONTRAST

How are the outer ear, middle ear, and inner ear alike? How are they different?

DESCRIBING SOUND

All sounds can be described as soft or loud, high or low, and pleasant or unpleasant. This is because every sound has several different properties. Scientists use systems of measurement to describe each property of sound.

"Intensity" is a word that is used to describe a sound's volume, or how soft or loud the sound is. Intensity is the

Strong vibrations are produced when a person shouts. Strong vibrations have great intensity and are loud.

People use a decibel meter to measure the loudness, or intensity, of sounds.

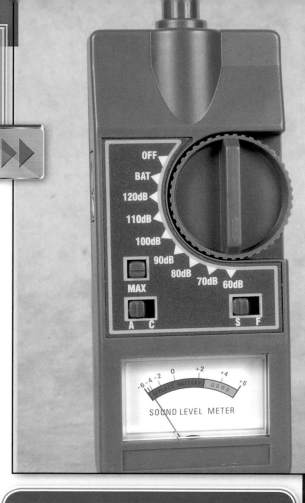

strength of the vibrations producing a sound. When a door is shut carefully, the vibrations made by that movement are weak and don't push the air with much force. This produces a quiet sound. When a door is slammed, strong vibrations are made. This creates a loud sound. Intensity is measured in decibels (dB). A measurement of 0 dB is the softest sound you can hear, while thunder measures at 120 dB.

Think About It

Would a police siren measure at a higher or lower number of decibels than a concert?

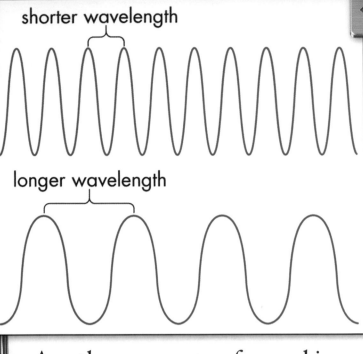

shorter wavelength

longer wavelength

◀◀

A shorter wavelength moves faster and causes a higher pitch than a longer wavelength does.

Vocabulary

Frequency is the number of complete vibrations per second.

Another property of sound is pitch. Pitch is how high or low a sound is. Faster vibration causes a higher pitch, while slower vibration causes a lower pitch. Wavelength, the distance from the peak of one wave to the peak of the next, is one way to measure vibration. Sounds with shorter wavelengths have a higher pitch and **frequency**. The unit of measurement used to record frequency is the hertz (Hz). One hertz is a complete vibration back and forth.

A woodpecker's call has a much higher pitch and many more vibrations per second than a cat's purr.

Sound waves travel at the same speed, no matter how quiet or loud they are. At room temperature, 70°F (21°C), sound travels 1,129 feet (334 meters) per second. That means that it takes sound about five seconds to travel 1 mile (1.6 kilometers). The warmer the air, the faster sound will travel. Sound waves travel even faster through water, metal, and stone.

Reflecting and Focusing Sound

Sound waves don't always go straight from the source to your ear. They can echo, or bounce off of other surfaces. This changes the way the sound is received.

Auditoriums are built to focus or strengthen sound. The shape and size of the room affects how sound reflects, or bounces around. Auditoriums usually have high, curved ceilings, and walls that move out at an angle

Vocabulary

Auditoriums are places where people see plays and listen to concerts.

An auditorium's shape determines how well sound travels throughout the room.

from the stage. Some have panels hanging from the ceiling to provide more surfaces for sound waves to bounce off.

When the source of a sound is moving, the sound changes. As the source of the sound, like an ambulance siren, gets closer to you, it sounds like it has a higher pitch. This is because the wavelengths are shortened. As it moves away, the wavelengths get longer, and so the pitch is lower. This is called the Doppler effect.

The Doppler Effect

with locomotive standing still, tone of whistle is normal

with locomotive approaching, whistle is high in pitch

with locomotive moving away, whistle is low in pitch

© 2013 Encyclopædia Britannica, Inc.

When the distance between a sound source and a listener changes, the the sound's pitch changes.

THE SOUND OF MUSIC

Musical instruments produce sound through vibration. Different types of instruments produce vibrations in different ways.

String instruments, such as violins, make sounds when a string is pulled, hit, or rubbed with a bow. The sound waves from the vibrating strings bounce around the inside of the body of the instrument. The pitch of the sound depends on how long the

The sound waves a violin makes bounce around inside of the body of the violin.

A drum kit can make a variety of sounds, with different pitches and intensities.

COMPARE AND CONTRAST

How are the sounds of these types of instruments the same? How are they different?

string is and the strength of the pull upon the string.

Flutes and other wind instruments create sound when air is blown into them. A flute player blows across an opening in a tube. The air that goes in the tube bounces around, producing sound.

Percussion instruments, such as drums, are hit to produce sound. The tightness of the drum skin, the size and shape of the drum, and how it is hit change what types of sounds are made.

CRANK IT UP!

As sound travels, it gets weaker. When we want sounds to reach a lot of people, we use something to amplify the sound, or make it louder. Two devices used to amplify sound are microphones and speakers.

A microphone is a receiver, like your ear. It picks up sound waves. When you speak or sing into a microphone, the sound waves hit a piece of material that captures vibrations. It then turns that sound energy into electrical energy, which can be delivered to a speaker.

A microphone lets a singer's voice reach thousands of listeners.

Microphones are found in telephones, computers, and hearing aids.

A speaker works the opposite way. The electrical energy caught by the microphone is changed back into vibrations through magnets. The magnets are attached to a cone-shaped piece. A good speaker will have different sized cones to reflect different frequencies of sound. Speakers are found in stereos, headphones, and televisions.

THINK ABOUT IT

In what situations might people need a way to amplify sound?

The speakers in these headphones turn electrical signals into music to enjoy.

CAPTURING SOUND

VOCABULARY

Audio is the sending, receiving, or reproducing of sound.

Sound recording, or **audio** recording, is the storage of sounds so that they can be heard again. In professional and home recording studios, people use special equipment to record music so that they can listen to it whenever they want.

Recording devices can preserve sound

Early phonographs recorded sound by marking a roll of tinfoil.

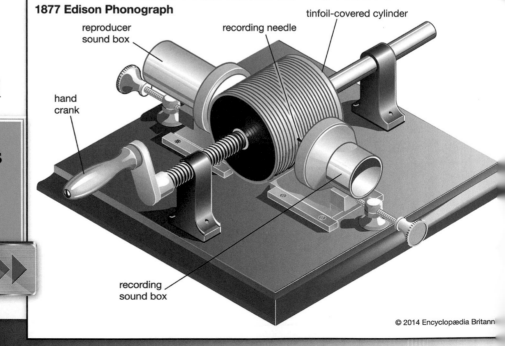

1877 Edison Phonograph

reproducer sound box

recording needle

tinfoil-covered cylinder

hand crank

recording sound box

© 2014 Encyclopædia Britann

in a number of formats. The earliest formats were phonograph records and magnetic tape. A phonograph record has a groove with patterns cut into it that represents the waves of sound. Magnetic tape represents sound with wavelike patterns of magnetized particles.

Most sound-recording devices today are digital devices. They store sound as a long series of numbers that describe the sound waves. CDs store this information as a pattern of tiny pits, or holes, that are created and read by a laser beam. These days digital information is most often stored in personal computers, phones, or portable devices called digital audio players.

Digital devices store and play large amounts of music as tiny files.

ANIMAL HEARING

Humans hear only certain frequencies. Some sounds are too high or low for us to hear because of how our ears are shaped. People can typically hear sounds between 20 and 20,000 Hz. A turtle can hear only between 20 and 1,000 Hz because it doesn't have outer ears. A dog or cat, on the other hand, can hear more than double

the range of frequencies we can. This is why they can tell when someone is coming to your door before they ring the bell.

Some animals use a process called echolocation to help them get around.

Mice can hear sounds between about 1 and 100,000 Hz.

COMPARE AND CONTRAST

How are a dog's ears like a person's? How are they different?

A bat makes a high-pitched noise while it flies, which people can't hear. The sound echoes back to the bat and helps it figure out how close it is to other objects. Bats use this information to avoid flying into things and to find food.

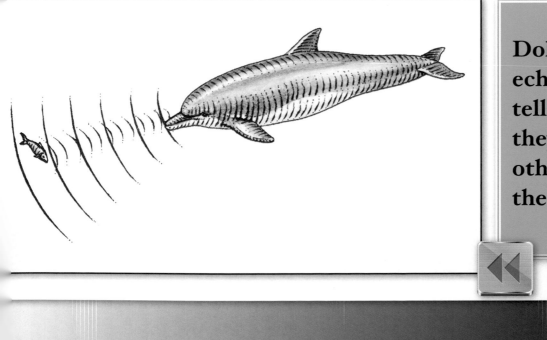

Dolphins use echolocation to tell how close they are to other objects in the ocean.

EXPLORING WITH SOUND

Humans have created a technology that mimics the echolocation ability that bats and other animals have. Sonar systems use sound waves to detect objects and figure out their size, their shape, and even how they are moving. Some systems send out the sound waves and pick up the reflections. Others receive sound waves sent by moving objects.

A military ship uses sonar to locate objects in the sea that may be dangerous.

Sailors on navy ships follow their sonar systems closely with computers.

The word "sonar" stands for "*so*und *na*vigation and *r*anging." Sonar technology is useful in situations where it is hard to see, such as underwater. In the ocean, sound waves can travel farther than light waves. Sonar can be used to study sea animals, find shipwrecks, and make maps of the ocean floor. Fishermen can use it to find large groups of fish to catch. The military can use it to detect enemy submarines before they can do harm.

THINK ABOUT IT

What could be some other uses for sonar technology?

SOUNDS IN MEDICINE

The sounds we cannot hear with our ears are useful to us in many ways. In medicine, doctors use a technology to produce sounds above 20,000 Hz called ultrasound. A special wand is used to send sound waves through the skin and into the body. The waves that reflect back are turned into a picture, so that the doctor can see what is inside the body. Ultrasound is used to detect

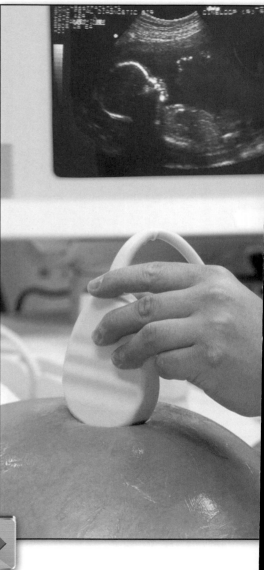

Doctors use ultrasound to see how a baby is forming inside a mother's body.

illnesses or examine babies before they are born.

Doctors are experimenting with ways to use sound to heal people, too. A new treatment uses high-frequency sound waves to kill certain types of cancer cells, with few side effects. Another treatment, called MIST, uses ultrasound waves pushed through salt water to help heal wounds that aren't getting better on their own.

THINK ABOUT IT

Why is it safer for a doctor to use ultrasound rather than to guess what is wrong with a patient or to perform surgery?

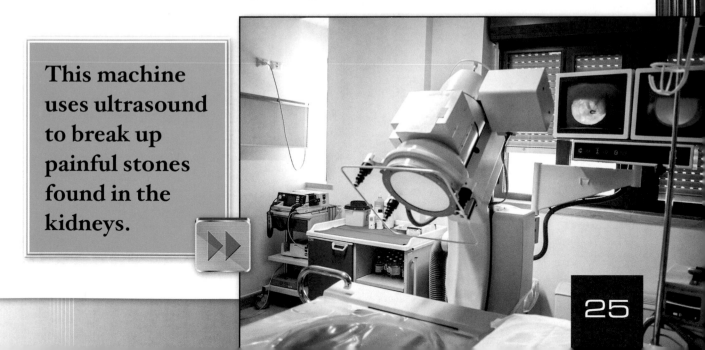

This machine uses ultrasound to break up painful stones found in the kidneys.

I Hear You

For most of history, people had to write letters to communicate with anyone far away. Beginning in 1876, people were able to talk to one another over great distances thanks to the telephone. The telephone can **transmit** sound over long distances.

When using a telephone, you speak into a microphone. Your voice is

Alexander Graham Bell, pictured here, invented the telephone in 1876.

> **VOCABULARY**
>
> To **transmit** is to send something.

Smartphones send and receive signals through the air as radio waves.

changed into an electrical signal and then sent to another phone. When the signal gets to the other phone, it is changed back into sound through a speaker.

Telephones have changed over time. In early phones, the signals were sent over a series of wires and cables. Now, signals can travel through the air as radio waves. Cell phones, combined with receiving towers and satellites, let people speak with one another from any place in the world. Wi-Fi (wireless fidelity) uses radio waves to transmit information at high speeds. It is how many people access the internet.

QUIET DOWN!

Sometimes, people want to reduce the noises they hear. When they do, they can use certain materials to absorb or block sounds. Fabrics, such as carpets or drapes, can absorb some sounds. Insulation in walls can block noise as well.

Noise pollution is a problem in big cities. Traffic and construction create lots of noise. Too much noise can make it difficult to sleep or concentrate and can even damage your hearing permanently. A sound at or above 120 dB is

Traffic causes noise pollution, bothering people who live nearby.

Construction workers often wear equipment to protect their hearing.

THINK ABOUT IT

What are some other ways to reduce noise pollution and hearing loss?

painful and can harm your ears. People who work with loud equipment usually wear earplugs to protect their hearing. When you use headphones, it's a good idea to keep the volume down. Once your hearing is impaired, it is very difficult to get it back.

Glossary

absorb To take in without giving back.

amplify To make greater or louder.

detect To discover or notice the presence of something.

echolocation A process used to find objects by projecting and receiving sound waves.

hertz A unit of frequency equal to one cycle per second.

impaired Hurt or damaged.

intensity Strength or force.

kinetic energy Moving energy.

laser beam A powerful beam of light.

medium An object or material through which sound energy travels.

mimic To imitate.

potential energy Energy that is stored.

produce To make.

property A special quality of a thing.

receiver A device that takes in a signal.

side effects Things that happen to your body because of a certain treatment that are not meant to happen.

source Where something comes from.

ultrasound Method of sending sound waves through something to see inside of it.

wavelength The distance in the line of advance of a wave from any one point to the next similar point.

FOR MORE INFORMATION

Books

Gardner, Robert. *A Kid's Book of Experiments with Sound*. New York, NY: Enslow Publishing, 2016.

Johnson, Robin. *The Science of Sound Waves*. New York, NY: Crabtree Publishing Company, 2017.

Shea, Therese. *How Dolphins and Other Animals Use Sonar*. New York, NY: PowerKids Press, 2014.

Spilsbury, Richard, and Louise Spilsbury. *Why Can't I Hear That? Pitch and Frequency*. Austin, TX: Raintree, 2014.

Winterberg, Jenna. *Sound Waves and Communication*. Huntington Beach, CA: Teacher Created Materials, 2015.

Websites

Because of the changing nature of internet links, Rosen Publishing has developed an online list of websites related to the subject of this book. This site is updated regularly. Please use this link to access the list:

http://www.rosenlinks.com/LFO/sound

INDEX